Praying Through it All

Encouraging words about motherhood, relationships, and faith

Brianna Baranowski
Copyright © 2024 Brianna Baranowski

All rights reserved.

ISBN: 979-8-8776-4691-9

DEDICATION

To my boys, and my man.

And also for my parents.

Brianna Baranowski

CONTENTS

Praying Through it All

Introduction

Revisiting this collection was a bit like traveling through time. There are stories of loss that bring the salty taste of tears back to my tongue. Pregnancy memories come with a fluttering, phantom kick inside my belly. From those first days of motherhood, where I didn't know what the heck was going on, to re-committing my life to Christ and finally finding peace again, these moments have come back to life in a beautifully bittersweet way. And I can't help it, I start to miss our old rocking chair.

That chair (actually a glider but let's not get caught up in semantics) was one of the first big purchases we made when preparing to bring our first son home. I remember sitting in it with my feet perched on the matching footstool, belly ballooned out and trying to imagine what this nursery would be like once the baby was here. Of course nothing could prepare me for the reality that lay ahead; one of immense, oxytocin-filled bliss blended with pure, sleep-deprived insanity, but it was nice to close my eyes, rock in the chair, and picture the future.

Throughout the next few years that chair was used more than any other piece of furniture in our home. I probably fell asleep in that chair just as many times as the boys did, often waking up with a trail of drool dripping from the corner of my mouth and a slight kink in my neck. But oh, the thoughts and dreams and prayers that came from that rocking chair. I worked out personal and family issues inside my head while rocking in that chair. When I noticed myself in a particularly whiny funk, I created the habit of thanking God for three specific things about each member of my family while rocking our youngest to sleep each night. We didn't go to church much during those early years of creating our family, but I held continuous worship in that chair.

In fact, no piece of baby nostalgia stung more to give away than that rocking chair. And that's saying something, because by the time I passed it down to my sister-in-law, it had seen better days. Breastmilk spills and toddler-adorned stickers covered the chair by the time it left our home. But that didn't matter, because that rocking chair is where life happened. It was where babies were soothed and prayers were answered and little boys climbed into my lap for story time. It was a quiet place to close my eyes for a moment and reflect a bit before putting a sleeping babe into his crib and sneaking out of his room. It was where I became born as a mother.

And so, even though my baby rocking days are gone, I've noticed that life still happens in the proximity of a rocking chair. It's sitting on the front porch with a friend, watching the kids run wild while sipping on some tea. It's the muscle memory of comforting a child by rocking them back and forth until their tears dry. It's savoring a sweet moment, being fully present with loved ones and feeling overwhelmingly grateful for the life you've been given. It's reflecting on a particular season of your life, and being transported back in time.

Motherhood

LETTING THE MILK GO BAD

BELLY TO BELLY

LAPS IN THE KITCHEN

HE NEEDED IT MORE

A BATH BOMB AIN'T GONNA CUT IT

TINY HANDS

PLAY PLACE LIMBO

SUGAR COOKIES

ELEMENTARY DEARS

LETTING THE MILK GO BAD

Our first child is due in eight days. The reality of this immediacy is met with the carton of milk sitting in our refrigerator, dated to expire after the baby's arrival. He will be here before the milk goes bad, for some reason that ignites eager anticipation through my husband and me. "Any day now," we're reminded, "any day now."

It's been a beautiful journey to get to this point, one so raw and primitive that I stop myself from fully engaging in the emotions, let alone writing them down. But today I will attempt to capture these fleeting moments in words, while my one cup of coffee ration cools beside me and life is quiet and still in our home. Perhaps it's not just our milk that has an expiration date, but our chapter as husband and wife alone as well.

I feel strangely guarded about our son. It could be that until I get to hold him in my arms he's still such an enigma in our lives. Perhaps it's my maternal instincts protecting him from the outside world. Maybe it's because I'm still navigating through the grief of our first pregnancy ending in loss. More likely than anything, I'm experiencing first time love and investment so commanding it's challenging to comprehend.

This child, a human already the size of a watermelon, will have a birthday soon. I always imagined that if I became pregnant, I'd go crazy not knowing what that baby would look like. It's funny how that detail can be so insignificant in reality. Because what I have come to know about him, what we've come to love, is enough. This little boy reassured me during the first few months with an extra dose of nausea any time I worried he wouldn't stick. When I would awaken from a nightmare about him, he'd kick me to let me know he was around. The way he playfully interacts with us in the womb, pushing out for his daddy and letting me tickle his little foot…his personality shines so bright. And when the doctor laughs at his movements and comments, "an active baby is a happy baby," I know what really matters.

And so, while we'll miss the sleepy Saturday mornings of idle companionship, we are ready for our baby boy. We will cherish these last few days of uncertainty regarding when labor will begin and what will transpire, because they are few. I'll sleep when I can and savor my marriage from this chapter of life while I can. My husband and I know that our relationship will evolve with our son's arrival, but at the end of the day we are ready for the milk to go bad.

Brianna Baranowski

BELLY TO BELLY

Inside my womb, little you began
the cord of life bonding us two.
Inside my belly, around you swam-
and from the start how we loved you.

Early morning when you arrived,
the doctor placed you upon my chest
Daddy smiled, he cut that cord-
we knew we loved you best.

Ten tiny fingers, long skinny toes,
so sleepy you could barely see.
I didn't know what I was doing,
but I knew you belonged to me.

You and I, we share a bond-
we snuggle skin to skin.
Those early days, always hungry-
drinking milk from within.

Belly to belly, my little bear,
both warm and soft are we.
How I cherish these early days-
rocking together, just you and me.

Now you're getting bigger,
almost one so soon.
Let's rock belly to belly, a little longer-
beneath the glowing moon.

LAPS IN THE KITCHEN

I know God hears me as I pace the kitchen at 3:00 in the morning, my newborn son nestled against my chest in the stretchy knit of a baby wrap. It's become our new routine, me groggy from a few weeks that have felt like one never-ending day, He faithful and encouraging.

I feel His presence wrap around me like the sling in which my sweet baby has found peace. It's not lost on me that like this baby so desperately needs to be settled down after a period of fussing and crying, I so desperately need these late night hours with God to be soothed by the one who loves me unconditionally.

As baby and I circle the kitchen island for the seventeenth time, He's here. He's with me while I silently exclaim my simultaneous gratitude, exhaustion, praise, and worry. I know He hears me while I mumble worship songs as lullabies, hushed so as not to wake the rest of the house.

It's become the only stillness in my day in a time when honestly I'm just trying to survive…

my C-section recovery, the wound still raw and sore

our first born still grappling with how rocked his little world has become

my husband still scrambling to support me when more often than not he's unsure how

and this tiny, precious, little miracle, still adjusting to life outside the warm embrace of the womb…

Nothing is figured out. Nothing is cohesive. Nothing seems certain. Nothing, that is, apart from my date with God at 3:00 AM.

He settles me down and walks me around, hushing and swaying in a soothing rhythm. He's reminding me that though sleeplessness is circumstantial, His faithfulness is forever. And in hearing Him, we walk on.

HE NEEDED IT MORE
Originally published on Motherly

It had been a day. The demanding, whining, limit pushing kind of day. The counting down until bedtime kind of day. You know, where you start fantasizing about how you'll spend your time once the kids are asleep? It was about forty minutes before bedtime, a Netflix marathon of Great British Baking Show dangling right in front of me, when I realized our toddler needed a bath.

There was no way we could push it back another night, we had already stretched those limits as it were. I started dreading the task, fully knowing he would fight it. I was low on energy and not sure I could summon the patience needed to pull this off.

I started thinking about how much I needed some self care, a bubble bath perhaps. After the day I had, I really needed a luxurious way to unwind and reset my mind. Then I looked at my sweet boy, genuinely struggling with his own emotions and burnout, and realized he needed it more.

You see, he had been fighting a virus that kicked his butt all week. His energy was drained and his emotions high. He didn't know that eventually he would feel like himself again, all he knew was in this moment he felt crappy and it might be like this forever.

Moreover, his teething baby brother was consuming most of mom's attention and time. His tank was running on empty, and the only way he could express that was through outbursts and tantrums. As the adage goes, "he wasn't giving me a hard time, he was having a hard time."

We often meet our children's nasty attitude with reaction rather than empathy. But in that moment I realized my ugliest moments are often met with God's strongest grace. And while I would have loved a spa worthy bubble bath experience, he needed it more.

He helped gather all the necessary supplies: bath bomb, candles, bubbles, a relaxing playlist. We dimmed the lights. I even dug around in his closet for the soft robe he got for Christmas last year. He practiced smelling the bath bomb's fragrance as it disintegrated into the water. It was altogether adorable and a little ridiculous. It was certainly 'extra,' but that's also my little guy, he's as extra as they come.

Eventually the mellow music was replaced by the Lion King soundtrack and the bubbles were popped with a splashing gusto, but for a few minutes our guest bathroom was transformed into a luxury spa. And after that bath, wrapped up in his robe and towel twisted atop his head, he smiled and hugged me. He may have needed that do-over, but I needed it more.

A BATH BOMB AIN'T GONNA CUT IT

I'm laying on the floor of our living room. Toys are strewn all about, and this house hasn't known silence for at least three years. I've convinced our toddler to play 'baby mama' which is basically when I pretend I'm a baby and he takes care of me. Right now it's baby mama's nap time. It's so sweet, he's set up a makeshift bed for me on the carpet complete with throw blankets and couch cushions. Our thirteen month old (no longer a baby but not quite a toddler just yet) is participating as best he can by climbing all over me and lovingly smacking my face. At this moment, they're content and having fun. But me, I know the reality. I'm completely aware of how much I've been phoning it in these last several weeks.

I used to pride myself on how energetic and engaged I was with my kids. I used to role play PJ Masks like nobody's business. You name the hero or villain, I have their catchphrases and mannerisms on lock! I've been the sultan of sensory, the princess of play...the queen of creative quiet time. But now, right now? I feel a bit like the mom character on any popular 90s sitcom: tired, nagging, looking to lie down a bit.

And look, it's not like I've been a total lazy bum, I just feel very much aware that I could be doing better with my kids. And the voice in my head reminds me I *should* be doing better with my kids. They're absolute delights (most of the time) and they deserve more than what I'm able to give right now. They deserve the whole dang moon and stars. They deserve a mom who's able to pull out some otherworldly strength from within and be constantly engaged with them. But I just don't have it in me right now.

If a friend were to confide in me this exact scenario, I know exactly what I would say to encourage her:

"Give yourself grace, mama!"

"You're doing great!"

"Have you been practicing self care?"

Of course there's so much more I would want to say, but these mantras of motherhood are always locked and loaded for my friends who are feeling down. They're the start of a conversation where the goal is to lift them up and provide comfort. So why do I struggle to say them to myself?

Give myself grace? I can barely extend grace to my husband and kids right now, there's none left for me.

I'm doing great? Are you kidding? My kid watched hours of TV today and the baby hasn't worn clothes other than pajamas for days. Come to think of it, neither have I…

Self Care?! Hahahahahahhahaa....a bath bomb ain't gonna cut it.

What I really need is a night without nursing, a day without diapers, perhaps a meal without "mama!" I need a chance to read a book or work on my writing without negotiating the terms with my husband. I need time with my friends without technology. I need face-to-face connection. I need to fill this empty cup that continues to pour regardless of the contents. I guess these are all examples of self care, but sometimes it's the shallow attempts of self care that are easiest to achieve.

I don't fault my family for any of this burnout. My kids are one and three, they don't understand the weight of this virus nor should they carry that burden. My husband is just as tired as I am, he's teaming up with me and balancing working from home. My parents are 1,800 miles away and my in-laws are high risk. We just need to soldier on, and hold onto hope. Hope that soon it'll be safe to invite friends over, or play with the neighbors. Hope that my job as a teacher won't be too negatively impacted by the time school starts again. Hope that I'll be back to my fully engaged self. Soon. And hope? It's a powerful tool.

So no, I'm not currently able to give all of myself to my kids *all* of the time. And I don't quite believe myself when I say that it's okay. But I'll keep saying it anyways. I'll keep saying it until I start to see the truth behind it. My kids may not have all of me all the time, but they have a father trying just as hard. They have each other. They have a dog for entertainment.

Heck, they have two pet tadpoles now thanks to an impulse purchase. They'll be okay. I'll be okay.

I will give myself grace.

I'm doing great.

I'll advocate for more self care. *Real* self care.

I'll be okay.

PLAY PLACE LIMBO

Welp, today we got stuck in one of those heinously overstimulating play places.

It started bleakly for us first timers from the start, just a mama grasping her wiggly 8 month old and traipsing behind her cautious toddler while he navigated the foreign territory. Of all days, we chose a snow day when all school-aged families decided to join the fun. Still, we forged ahead.

A few minutes in and levels up, it became apparent that the longest slide was the happening place to be. My toddler was determined. Never one to leave a man behind, the baby and I followed. Climbing over hurdles, crawling through tight tunnels, ducking from other children, our expedition felt finished when we finally made it to the top.

Only, he changed his mind about the slide. Too big. Too scary. Totally understandable. A crowd was forming behind us and we decided to find a new way back down. The only exit other than the slide: a teeny crawl space that just wasn't gonna happen for me and baby. I was about to suggest we go back down the way we came, when my toddler was found on the other end of the tiny crawl space. Uh oh. We've been separated.

The never-ending music and echoes of delighted screams drowned out my directions for him to come back. He looked panicked, and continued down a different path. It felt like 100 degrees in this netted canopy, and despite the bitter cold outside I was sweating through my clothes. So loud. So hot. So far away from my big boy who's really still a baby. We forged on.

Eventually, after what felt like an eternity, we were reunited. The relief was palpable. He wanted to keep playing, I wanted to get.the.heck.outta.there.

Crawling out of that fever dream playscape, I looked down. Shoot, the baby had lost a sock. It must've fallen off in one of the tunnels. Shaking my head, we forged on.

I may never leave a man behind, but I'll count my losses on a stranded sock any day.

TINY HANDS
Originally published on Her View from Home

We're swaying to the steady rhythm of the rocking chair, a nestled buoy bobbing with the current. My sweet baby boy, how you've already changed so much in these few short months. It's in this chair that time seems to freeze and fly in varying waves of realization. Breaking free from the blanket in a gentle act of rebellion, your hands reach for me. They're dimpled, tiny, and perfect. They're the simplest marker of time, your hands.

Those hands that splayed your fingers wide and long as the doctor pulled you from my body. I'll never forget, against all the drugs working through my veins for the surgery, the clarity in which I saw those hands. Those hands that searched and reached for my face when finally, *finally*, they brought you to me on the operating table. How long your fingernails were on those wrinkly hands! Already I miss those hands.

Those hands that were clenched fists during the first weeks. Struggling with feedings and trying to get to know one another, your hands acted as my indicator of when you were full. I'd carefully watch those hands tighten and relax and felt reassured we'd be okay. They sometimes made me nervous, those hands.

Newborn you would squeeze your daddy's finger with those hands. I'd watch as his eyes lit up and his heart swelled to twice its size each time you grabbed with those little hands. Slowly they learned how to explore your face and my hair and the dog...so primitive and yet so engaged were those hands.

Now you're seven months old and I wish we could slow down, baby boy. Each day you amaze me, along with those hands. They're a fast paced succession of exploration, constantly reaching and grasping. You light up as you learn to wave, to sign, to *communicate* with those hands. And yet, this is just the beginning.

As we rock together, and your eyes become heavy, I think about the future of those hands.

Hands that will make colorful art, covered in paint.

Hands that will play in dirt and pull long, juicy earthworms from the ground.

Hands that will sometimes hit and push and refuse to share.

Hands that will wrap around us in tight hugs.

Hands that will write your sweet little name on the top right corner of a piece of paper.

Hands that will play catch with your big brother and daddy.

Hands that will come together in prayer before bed each night.

Hands that will make friends with an initial high five or fist bump.

Hands that will one day grow the courage to call (or text) a girl.

Hands that will learn the meaning of hard work and one day find their purpose in this life.

Hands that are no longer dimpled and tiny, but will always be perfect to me. Son, you won't always reach for me in the dead of night. I won't always be your buoy to steady the current. But know this, I will always ALWAYS love you and those hands.

SUGAR COOKIES

"Mommy, I eat it?"

"No, honey, that's just butter. It's yucky by itself," I replied, much to his disappointment.

We turned the stand mixer back on and prepared the next few ingredients. As we cracked the eggs, their whites running down his dimpled hands, my two year old asked again, "Mommy, I eat it?"

"Not the eggs, hun. They'll make you sick before they're cooked." His brow furrowed at me but he resisted the urge to rebel. We washed our hands.

And then I noticed the pattern of what it really takes to make these sugar cut-out cookies: a lot of ingredients that individually are frankly pretty gross until they're blended, baked, and decorated to our delight.

Having baked these cookies with my mom since I was a kid, I could see the outcome before it arrived. I knew that with a little patience and diligence, we'd soon be enjoying these Christmas cookies together. It was so clear to me.

It was not so clear, however, to my toddler who was losing his patience and self control by the minute. As far as he was concerned, I was denying him the objects of his desire. Vanilla extract, oh how he wanted to eat the vanilla extract! But mom said no. Raw flour, sifted and floating all around us? Still mom said to wait a little longer.

I wonder how many times I've viewed life through this short-sighted lens? How many times I've crumbled after a disappointment, unwilling or unable to see the bigger picture. The break ups, the missed opportunities, the "dream jobs" I never landed? How disastrous they felt in the moment! But all along, there was a whisper I didn't want to hear, "Just a little longer, your life is meant for more."

There are parts of our lives that may leave us with a bitter taste in our mouths, but if we hold out a little longer, and trust the process, how sweet it could become.

ELEMENTARY, MY DEARS

Suddenly, there are stray Nerf bullets found in my washing machine drum.

The other night, a tender moment and sweet hug lead to the loudest fart I've ever heard.

Right before bed, my living room transforms into WWE every night.

It can only mean one thing- it's elementary, my dear.

I'm parenting within the early elementary years. We're knee-deep in knock knock jokes and at the precipice of puns. The kids are growing up, but they haven't developed their preteen 'tudes yet. Okay, maybe the attitudes have already started to shine, but I'm prepared for them to get a lot worse! And though it may seem chaotic and smelly at times, I can be honest with myself and admit that this is quickly becoming my favorite chapter of motherhood yet.

Though rocking a sleepy newborn was divine, and exchanging inquiries with a toddler is adorable, I'm absolutely cherishing this window of time with my young-ish boys.

It's teaching them how to read, subtract, and play chess. And then trying not to take it personally when their queen takes my bishop.

It's them asking big questions and not settling for anything less than a big, in-depth answer. No, but really, how do airplanes manage to stay in the sky? Because Bernoulli's Principle was definitely not covered in any of my college classes.

It's still getting to snuggle with my boys, even if it now means I gotta catch them first thing in the morning or when they're not feeling well.

It's finally having learned all the names of the dinosaurs, only to discover it's all about Pokemon now and there is an infinite number of them.

It's my inner child screaming in delight as I realize all my childhood favorites are popular again (hello, Power Rangers! And TMNT! And Razor Scooters!), and I get to play with them all!

It's watching them develop meaningful friendships, all on their own.

Elementary years are grass stains before pit stains, potty humor before it gets too outta hand, and brotherly love before they get sick of each other (tell me they'll just always love each other this much, though, okay?).

It's hard to admit, my husband and I are not 'baby' people. So it's entirely possible that our earlier struggles with parenthood are just feeling all the more sweet now that our kids are a little older and more independent. But let me tell you, we're basking in it. We lay in bed at night and gush about the boys: their triumphs, the cute way they both say Netflix (netflist), or just any little detail about their day. We share those moments with each other and then heave a collective exhale of relief. Everyone who encouraged us was right- it *does* get easier and better.

Getting through the fog that enveloped me the first few years of motherhood sometimes has me wishing I could go back in time with clearer vision. I'd worry less, and certainly soak it in more. But I also recognize the ease of which this season brings, and it strengthens me to never take it for granted.

And so it is with great appreciation and joy that I soak up these frog-catching, trampoline-jumping, rocket-launching years. I will hug and hold onto my sweet, silly, elementary dears.

Brianna Baranowski

Praying Through it All

Faith

A MOTHER'S LOVE SHOULD BE RECKLESS

GOD, HELP ME LOVE THEM WELL

BE STILL

ARCHITECT OF MY LIFE

EARLY TO CHURCH

A MOTHER'S LOVE SHOULD BE RECKLESS

"Reckless Love" by Cory Asbury is a song that seems to serendipitously surprise me at the right moment, randomly playing on the radio like an anthem I desperately need. It began about a year ago, and I immediately had this overwhelming confidence that God wanted me to pay attention to this song and its meaning.

Like I'm sure many of you do, I struggle with the weight of God's "overwhelming, never-ending, reckless love." I don't doubt it, but it's difficult for me to accept this vast kind of love that I cannot earn and definitely don't deserve. Surely my mistakes and misgivings chip away at this supposed unconditional love, right? Despite my uncertainty there was this nudge to breathe in the song each time it played. In conversation with my husband I referred to it as 'my song.' But what was the purpose?

The purpose wasn't clear to me until last week. It was a Thursday morning, a *tough* Thursday morning. We hadn't left the house in two days, and I was beginning to feel like a failure. The house was a mess, we had been staying in our pajamas, and I was feeling run down from a week of accruing sleep debt.

I was desperate to get the kids and myself out of the house, but inclement winter weather and a semi-rigid baby nap schedule made our opportunities slim to seize. I began to brainstorm. What was something quick and easy we could manage this manic morning, bonus points if we could all stay in our pajamas? The Dunkin' Donuts drive thru! The possibility of an extra dose of caffeine was just icing on the sprinkle donut. My two year old would be ecstatic, we rarely ever indulge in such a treat.

He refused. What?! Like who refuses a donut? He insisted he wanted to stay home, again. While I was flattered we've managed to make our home such a sanctuary to him, it was starting to feel to me more like house arrest. But I wasn't about to fight him on behalf of a guilty pleasure, so we stayed home and did art instead.

Later, during that impossibly tight window between lunch and nap I tried my hand at fate once more. I felt like Anna trying to persuade Elsa, "Do you wanna get a donutttttt?" "Um, sure. Let's do it," he replied nonchalantly. Great. Let's get the baby in his carseat and bust outta here.

My toddler began whining for a snack before we left the garage.

"Buddy, it's a two minute drive to Dunkin' Donuts."
"I want a snaaaaaaaack!"
"Um, okay, here's some goldfish."
"No goldfish!"
"Okay."
"Yes goldfish!"

I lost my patience. Did I mention we hadn't backed out the garage yet? "If you keep whining I'm going to buy myself a donut and you won't get anything!" I didn't-quite-but-basically-yelled. The SUV was quiet, but it was far from peace and quiet. I've never been one to use threats, and the wave of guilt knocked me down immediately.

Wanting a musical escape, I turned on the radio for our quick commute. My song. I couldn't believe it. I turned it up a little louder. After a morning of feeling like a total loser I needed that message with incredible urgency. More than that, my precious little boy needed the message that unconditional love "chases (him) down, fights 'til (he's) found, leaves the ninety-nine."

"Don't deserve it," I heard my two year old repeat. Hmmm...he doesn't usually pay attention to song lyrics. He said something else that I couldn't hear.

"What was that, honey?"

"I was sad and this song made me feel better." His voice was sweet and pensive.

"I like this song too."

"I love it."

There was the nudge. Have I ever talked to my son about God's love? Did he fully know about my unconditional love for him?

"You know hun, this song is about how God loves us no matter what, even if we're angry or sad or tired or cranky. He still loves us. And even though I might get frustrated sometimes, I love you no matter what. I'm sorry you were feeling sad. I love you so much."

And my beautiful boy, so wise beyond his two years, nodded his head and smiled.

"We're at the donut place!"

And we were. In the two minutes it took to reach our destination, I was able to disciple to my child in a meaningful way. It was one of the most precious, fulfilling, purpose-driven moments of my life.

GOD, HELP ME LOVE THEM WELL

God, help me love them well.

On our best days, when I'm overwhelmed with gratitude.
On our worst days, when I'm just...overwhelmed.
On our mediocre days, when I'm left feeling like I'm not enough.

Remind me to see the bigger picture by viewing these precious gifts through a wider lens.

Help me love them well.

When they're silly and our home is filled with infectious belly laughs.
When they're sweet and their hugs radiate through my body and into my soul.
When they're needy and leave me wanting just one minute to myself.
Remind me to count it all joy.

Help me love them well.
Give me patience, when anger begins to feed.
Give me strength, to be everything they need.
Give me wisdom, to plant that mustard seed.

And God? Thanks for loving me well.

BE STILL

All these running thoughts inside of me
Lord I'm paralyzed with anxiety
I know that you have better plans for me
and really all you're asking me is to **be still**

I know this fear's not part of your will
God quiet all this chaotic outside noise
keep me focused on you, my boys
help me lift my eyes and **be still**

So much is unknown right now
I know we can recover but not sure how
this season seems too steep a hill
but instead of climb you ask I only **be still**

Lord you're my refuge and my strength
while I'm sheltered here in place
I want to be strong for my family
so I'll find comfort and I'll heed your plea

Give me peace and give me guidance
help me share your love and kindness
worry and fear say I'll never have my fill
but I'll smile, take a breath, and **be still**

EARLY TO CHURCH

Sometimes I barge into the service while the first worship song is already playing, awkwardly excusing myself while shimmying into an empty chair after tossing the kids into their Sunday school classroom like a hand grenade.

Mind you, this is the late service. By now we've been up for hours but still managed to be tardy to the party. But let's face it, at 10:15 we've practically lived out an entire day already!

But, ah. Sometimes we dress and brush and buckle at a speed less resembling a sloth (AKA the first time being asked). We're not only on time, we're miraculously early. The kids can walk into their classroom without the frenetic frenzy of the Sunday rush.

And on those beautifully rare days, I have time to throw a buck into the basket and pour myself a free-will donation cup of coffee. I get to choose from a delectable variety of flavored creamers, a luxury we don't keep at home. I small talk with a few fellow church members and stir my coffee with one of those mini little straw things.

I practically float into the sanctuary. It's still pretty empty, so I have my pick of seats (always the far right side, I'm not exactly sure why). I let out a contented exhale while watching the announcement screen and listening to the band warm up and again, I savor a sip. Ah, the coffee is still warm. In fact, every ounce of that styrofoam cup will remain warm- no multiple microwave zapping required.

I enjoy church just as much on the running late, coffee-free Sundays that tend to be my norm. The spirit swells my heart during worship all the same. But ah, those Sunday mornings when I can sit in peace and drink that cup of coffee, those mornings are magic.

ARCHITECT OF MY LIFE

Time and time again God's plan for my life reveals itself when I least expect it. Pieces seem to fall perfectly into place, the fog lifts from my uncertainty, and my brain thinks something along the lines of, "Oh, right, *that's* how it's supposed to go." It's as if behind the scenes there's a beautifully orchestrated blueprint being followed down to the exact angle of every corner. Thankfully, I tend to have little to nothing to do with it.

That's because God is the architect of my life. He has carefully and meticulously had a hand in every lesson and step in my journey.

Every broken heart, rejection, and career slump has led me to something bigger than I could have imagined for myself. And while sometimes that bigger thing is just a lesson that I needed to learn, I've come out the other side better because of it.

But it's hard to remember who has their hand in our lives when we're in the midst of waiting or a period of what feels like continuous rejection. In fact, mere moments ago this morning, I received an email notifying me about yet another job I wasn't going to be hired for. And despite my faith in God, I let myself feel the crushing disappointment once again, if only for a moment.

I can't wallow in my self-pity for too long, not when I know just how short-sighted I can be when it comes to the great commission and true purpose of my life. I will wipe my tears, take a deep breath, and open my Bible back up to Romans 8:28, "And we know that in all things God works for the good of those who love him, who have been called according to his purpose."

He works for the good of me. I might not see it now, or tomorrow, or a year from now, but He is walking with me during this season of waiting and rejection. I will trust in Him, for He is truly the architect of my life.

Praying Through it All

Marriage

IMPORTED

FIND ME

BREATHLESS WONDER

LOVE AND ACCEPTANCE

I'VE CHANGED MY MIND ABOUT EVERYTHING
BUT YOU

IMPORTED

Somewhere between Kinnick Stadium and a case of Busch Light, I found myself an assimilated Iowan. This cognizance emerged last week when I invited friends to a 'grill out' instead of a 'barbeque;' the shift in dialect was unperceived to everyone but me. It was sudden and it was scary and I knew I could no longer rely on the crutch of being a California girl.

This emanation into Midwest living transpired after surviving what I have been assured was an unusually atrocious winter. For months those I met would pat my back in a display of solidarity, consoling, "it's not normally like this, this is the worst winter in years!" My fiancé and I would exchange a secret smile each time we were comforted by the supposed mantra of the locals. They must not realize that to me, the polar vortexes and freezing rain and squalls were the breathing, fibrous proof that I was alive.

The everyday doldrums of the Golden State remain a constant. It didn't matter the season, I was sure to be greeted with a plastic existence of sunny and 75. Driving through the neighborhoods of Orange County, streets are littered with orderly, uniformed palm trees. Palms are not native to California, and their fraudulent presence is a reminder that nothing here is true. But that was all I knew for twenty-five years, and I would relish in the sameness of each passing day: the crawling commute on the 405, the splattering of freckles on my sun-kissed skin, the way I'd fret over driving in the rare occurrence of a rain shower. Until recently, I assumed my life was enviable and unchanging.

And then I fell in love, as what happens in most of life's testaments. He was handsome and ambitious and hygienic. Sure, basic hygiene is typically assumed, but keep in mind I grew up in the land of apparent endless waves, summer, and days without showering.

His name was Ryan and immediately I coined him as different from my dating schema (a huge plus). He was from the previously unascertained land of Chicago. The night we met I confessed I thought the two Chicago baseball teams were the White and Red Sox. Looking back, this unhealthily obsessed Cubs fan must have been extremely smitten to not walk away right then and there. It is something I'm embarrassed about now, but what can I say? Water polo and swimming were way more popular to me than baseball.

This Midwest man with his charms and goals forgave my naivety, and we began to share a life together. Three years and one professorship later, this life included the 1,800-mile relocation to Cedar Rapids, Iowa. Assuming I would hate the location but support the man, my geographical expectations were dismal. I mean, I was leaving the land where all dreams are realized through motion picture. I carried myself as a saint those last few months before our move, allowing Ryan to exalt me for making the ultimate sacrifice. I felt utterly commendable.

It took five days in a two-door Honda to reach our new city. By the time we hit Zion, Utah, my self-centered skin began to shed. Towering above us were daunting rock formations whose diverse geological layers served as the story of time. We hiked up some of these mountains, as ill prepared in our flip-flops as we undoubtedly were for this new adventure. We lodged in cabins. We treated ourselves to a steak dinner. The road trip was a whirlwind of miles, each day boasting a new part of the country. I could no longer see the Pacific Ocean, but I did see The Rocky Mountains, a gun show in Cheyenne, an expanse of possibilities.

My first impression of Iowa that July was, buzzing. The buzzing of gnats and the way their impenetrable swarm so closely hugged the outfield lights at Ryan's softball games, the visceral irritation they brought as they flitted around my nose, my eyes, my throat like a bad cough that refused to shake. The buzzing of energy in the mornings, when I'd sit on my patio and listen to the birds and cicadas and whatever else was making all that noise. The bustling of going out with new friends and learning very quickly that this was a town that knew how to get a buzz going, everything seemed to reverberate with the sweet sounds of summer.

I still giggle a little when people refer to soda as 'pop,' and I will always grumble about the cost of avocados at Hy-Vee, but my year in Iowa has been one of trying new things. I am now learned in the art of tailgating before a hawks game, waking up and heading out to Kinnick as if to chase the rising sun to The Hill. I know what a pork tenderloin sandwich is, though I still sometimes crave carne asada. When winter hit and I was not sure it would ever end, I purchased my very first set of long underwear. Yes, sometimes I miss home, but there are days I drive on 380, marvel at the stretch of uninterrupted tableau, and don't miss the palm trees at all.

FIND ME

A three bedroom house with a fireplace
is empty and bare
unless we share the space.
We roam and we walk but we're misplaced-
then you come and you find me.
Oh, you're the anchor and I'm the sea,
you had to reach but you steadied me.
And I'd give anything to need nothing
but you come and you find me.

BREATHLESS WONDER

May we always go outside to soak up a gorgeous sky. To really take it in, breathless in wonder.

May our feet always find their way to each other under layers of blankets. Even when cocooned in slumber we're connected on the smallest scale.

May our gaze always meet to share a secret smirk amidst the chaos of our bustling home. They may be the monkeys and our home a circus, but at least we get to lead the ring.

May we always offer the other coffee, a gesture that's the powerful tiller of this ship. A topped off mug procured to our tastes is the ultimate love language.

And may we always remember to soak up one another while admiring that gorgeous sky, breathless in wonder.

LOVE AND ACCEPTANCE

I'm thankful to have my husband. He may not be the most romantic or intuitive of spouses, but darn if he doesn't wholly accept me for who I am (not who I once was or who I could become). In fact, he's so shockingly understanding that I often struggle accepting his acceptance.

Does that make sense? Like, I've become so accustomed to people trying to change or 'fix' me when I share my feelings that when Ryan listens there's a part of me convinced that he must be hiding his true thoughts. He must think I'm too much, he's certainly going to leave me one day. That part of me, the shame associated with my own self, fears he's keeping a record of every off-putting confession I've ever spoken, until one day I discover he's met his 'crazy quota' and is done with me. But since that hasn't happened yet, it's safe to assume his quota must be limitless. And the part of me who is slowly becoming more self-loving recognizes that he's just that great of a man. And I'm worthy of his love and acceptance.

Don't get me wrong, I deeply and strongly value the relationships established with my family and girlfriends. Truthfully, I am comfortable being honest about the highs and lows of my life with most people. But often those conversations have my palms sweating and my inner voice screeching how poorly I'm attempting to articulate my feelings.

It's honesty with a side of self doubt. And it's nothing against my friends, either. I just recognize that the core of intimacy at its most vulnerable and rare is what I feel with Ryan. He's my lifeline, my rescue unit. And that's what I hope for everyone. Find someone to be your safe place. Someone to pull you from the wreckage with a first aid kit of a warm beverage, genuinely comforting hug, and (most importantly) an ear free from judgement. You will absolutely need this person, whether it's a partner or friend, because in the throes of new parenthood you'll want and need to be your truly authentic self without the mask of keeping it neat and together. Find that person and cherish them deeply. Better yet, find that person and condition yourself to be that kind of lifeline in return.

I'VE CHANGED MY MIND ABOUT EVERYTHING BUT YOU
Originally published on Her View from Home

When I was a little girl, I couldn't pick my favorite Spice Girl. I loved Baby Spice, but was also a big fan of sports. So what about Sporty Spice? And all their outfits were so cool, I couldn't make up my mind about which one I hoped to become one day.

When I was in middle school, I'd eagerly await my bi-weekly orthodontist appointments just so I could pick a new band color for my braces. And within a day or two, I'd have already decided I hated them, and would impatiently wait for the next time they could be changed.

In high school, my parents went from my best friends, to my antagonists, and back to baseline all within a 24 hour period. Repeat every day for four years.

And in college, my major changed more often than my Jeep's air freshener.

Let's just say it this way- nobody is nominating me for "Most Loyal" or "Miss Steadfast" anytime soon. I've just always been one to change my mind about things. Jobs, personal style, heck, even (maybe *especially* is more like it) dating was no exception. I'd fall in love, all googly eyed and writing his name in cursive over and over again in my notebook, and then, like clockwork, the sun would stop shining out of his butt. There'd be minor annoyances that grew into big ones, or beige flags that started to look more red, or major deal breakers that I was blind to in the beginning but unable to ignore any longer. There'd always be *something* that made me want to retreat. Often, I'd break-up with a boyfriend only to get back together again a few weeks later. Then, you guessed it, we'd break up again.

I'm not proud to admit this, but I kind of sucked at dating until I met you.

But you appeared before me at the bar with confidence that never broached towards arrogance. Right away, I knew you were in a different league altogether from anyone else I'd ever even spoken with. Your green eyes shimmered as you thirsted for more details about me, and I reciprocated from drinking in all I could learn about you. The night we met, I went home and immediately forgot what your face looked like. It was more of a shift in my entire perspective that stuck with me. I was so scared I was going to screw it all up.

At our six month dating milestone, I admitted that I'd never consecutively dated anyone that long without at least one 'break.' You asked me why that was, and I remember shrugging, "I just usually get sick of someone before then." I applaud you for not running away right then and there. And I'm proud of myself for sticking around, too.

Over thirteen years we've made the decision to choose each other. And even if all those seven million-ish minutes weren't always magical, they've been so worth sticking around for. *You,* have been worth sticking around for.

Family and Friends

DAUGHTER OF A DREAMER

SUNSHINE

MONARCHS

NOT ALL HABITS ARE BAD

LONG-DISTANCE GRANDPARENTS

MADE FOR THIS

GIVE ME FRIENDS WHO AREN'T KEEPING UP
WITH THE JONESES

HOSTESS WITHOUT THE MOSTEST

DAUGHTER OF A DREAMER
Written before my wedding

Forget the 'vintage inspired' dress, the heinously expensive out-of-season peonies (but they bring so much whimsy!) and the hopeless hours perusing Etsy for something both affordable *and* unique, as my wedding began to loom heavier on my shoulders and those doubts you aren't supposed to address started to rise, my biggest worry was wolves.

My dad never seemed concerned about not knowing his biological father. I'd berate him constantly to do one of those ancestry searches on the internet (I mean, come on, that's fifty percent of your genetic makeup unknown) to no avail. This really bothered me, and rang an alarm over a multitude of things. Selfishly speaking, that's a quarter of my life that is a mystery. What if there's a history of cancer, or male pattern baldness? My god, is there such a thing as female pattern baldness? Perhaps as a stifled coping mechanism (how can he not be at least curious?), my dad had a penchant for claiming our family of four as our own pack. There never was an official motto, but if there was I imagine it'd go something like, 'We are the Ecks, our name may be strange and there may not be many of us, but we are united!'

He is so proud of our little pack that when I was nine my dad started 'howling' at the moon each time our family was outside at night together. I'm not sure I can convey how extremely self conscious I can be (though for a visual I still pick apart my sandwiches with my hands to avoid food particles getting stuck in my teeth, a trait picked up from about a thousand years of orthodontic wear. I take no chances.), so take my word that it was horrifying. We'd be strolling along the damp sand in Huntington Beach, California, parallel with the incoming tide and letting the exhausted tip of a wave brush against our bare feet, and out of nowhere he'd let out a wolflike howl, nudging my brother Tyler and I to join in on the sudden lunacy. I don't remember my mom ever being cajoled into howling, but perhaps because she wasn't technically a blood Eck, just the married into kind. Tyler, younger and more pliable, would let out a cub whimper and then cower into silence, giggling to himself. I wasn't about to do anything self-deprecating, all the more stubborn since anything my dad initiated during those years was met with resistance.

The glow of the moon was a spotlight on my nine year old scowl. Sure, it'd be fun to howl like a crazy person, freeing even. But we were in public! My early onset spinsterness found it wildly inappropriate to behave like an animal whilst in the eye of four, maybe five other beach walkers. And as demonstrated on so many of my favorite television shows, wasn't taking a walk on the beach the setting for 90% of romantic dates? Who were we to ruin somebody's magical night? I rolled my eyes aggressively with the aim that my dad could see it by his beloved moon's light. This only prompted him to grin that forever childlike grin and embarrass me more.

Our conversation went something like this:

Dad: Come on, hun! You're an Eck! Be proud! (insert obnoxious howling here)

Me: You're insane, can we go home now?

Dad: Nope, not until my cub proclaims herself as a member of our pack.

Me: One day I'm putting you in a home. (insert one more eye roll, for good measure)

Dad: Brianna, you're nine, get over yourself. Just try it.

Me: Fine. (clears throat, reluctantly looks up at night sky, howls sheepishly)

Dad: That's my baby girl! Eck pack, united!

Me: (Howls at moon with more fervor, overcome by temporary lunacy and the thrill of not giving a hoot).

. . .

Over the years, this scene would replay in different settings. Perhaps while walking into a movie theater, or after leaving a family event, sometimes we would engage in this silly ritual after having just watered the front lawn together. Wherever it was, my dad would always initiate and I always reluctantly joined in. That's just how we did things in most situations. My dad carries a knack for being free and fun, and I'm the grump that needs convincing.

It was on a recent vacation to Savannah, Georgia that my wedding worries sunk in. The four of us were there together, after three months of me living in Iowa (and away from them for the first time ever). My fiance Ryan couldn't make the Savannah trip because he had to teach that week, and so it was a fluke that this vacation consisted only of the original four. We were roaming the cobblestone streets of Riverwalk Boulevard, perusing the candy shops and attempting to emulate the sweet drawls of the locals. I was a mess because I thought wearing three inch wedges was somehow a good idea, and my family bursted into laughter each time I stumbled over the hundreds year old stones. Through cursing at myself, I laughed along with them.

Tripping along behind the other three, I noticed my dad stop suddenly. Across the street was a burly man dressed in a tattered basketball jersey and stained sweatpants. Without the aid of any instrument he was belting out the Christian classic, "This Little Light of Mine." His rendition was soulful and echoed beyond the shops and tourists. It could baptize the soul just by permeating your eardrums. Tears were forming, though not escaping my dad's eyes (he's not one to shy away from an occasional cry). This was one of those moments for him, the kind that reminds him how rare it will be from now on for just the four of us to spend time together. I can always tell when one of those moments rises into my dad's mind; he gets this pitiful look that yearns for those early years back. Twenty-six and now longer succumbed to the fear of what strangers might think, I smiled meekly at him and pointed up. Looming large was a full moon, most likely the same one that inspired the Savannah song,

"Moon River." He smiled back at me, and let out a howl. Without needing a nudge, the rest of us followed suit. I couldn't tell you what the passerby crowd was thinking when they saw this strange distraction, I didn't bother to look around.

So now, a few months away from being married, I worry about wolves. I worry that by becoming part of another family, I'll lose some of the closeness I already share with my own. I worry that if I take my husband's name, I'll lose what it means to be an Eck. But mostly, I worry that I'll forget how to howl at the moon.

SUNSHINE

When I was a little girl, I was raised on loving words. Inner confidence bloomed inside of me like a sunflower, ever tilting and rotating towards the light.

That light was (and still is) my grandma.

My grandma beams when I walk into a room. I can remember from my earliest years the way she would embrace me and make sure I felt like the most beautiful thing she had ever laid eyes on. When I was young, she'd take me shopping and say things like, "Well sweetheart, you just look so good in everything you try on. I guess we have to buy it all." She'd sing *You are my Sunshine* to me when I visited her home, making me feel incredibly special.

As an adult, she notices things like highlights in my hair, or a new nail polish color I'm trying out. She is, and has always been, a beacon of light that chases away the shadowy tendrils of my inner critic.

I know this will sound entitled, but for years I wrestled with this kind of admiration. For one, I'm not someone who invests a lot into how I look. I've had my tomboy, my low-maintenance, and my 'unfortunate experiments on my hair' phases. I didn't like such an emphasis on outward appearances, especially in the early throes of new motherhood when I already felt raw and exposed. So for a few years, I'd come to reject or secretly resent her attention to me, even when complimentary.

But I've since learned that this is about more than body image or fashion. It's perhaps about my grandma healing her inner wounded child through me. It's her loving me when loving herself feels impossible. It's about her making sure that crippling negativity doesn't carry on to the next generation.

My grandma has never been as kind to herself as she's been to me. She calls herself names out loud, and I know they're not nearly as bad as the ones she's thinking on the inside. There's never been a holiday or special event when she stepped out in bold confidence as the striking force she happens to be. Instead of the sunflower she's raised me to be, she's more of a shade-seeking flower, shying from the sun.

I'm not sure if this low self-esteem is generational, or due to the trauma I know she endured, or the result of a negative man who abruptly left their marriage after several decades. It's probably a combination of many heartbreaking things. What I do know is that she struggles to live with an inner critic so harsh, it diminishes the wonderful things about this woman.

This woman, who pulled herself out of poverty. This woman who found love again after it felt lost forever. This woman, who has persisted through several back surgeries, chronic pain, and severe hearing loss. This woman, who is a noble matriarch in our family. This woman, who taught us about Jesus. She doesn't love herself as she should. As she deserves.

I can see now why she showers me with adoration. It's clear why she tells me I'm her sunshine. And it's definitely never been about me being particularly great in any way. Because trust me, I'm not. I'm a perfectly imperfect work in progress.

No, her heavy handed love for me is because she doesn't want me to live my life carrying self-doubt and insecurity. She doesn't want me to live in the dark. She carries those things, but she doesn't want to pass along the shadows to me.

Her love is a flashlight, and it shines bright.

My grandma is now almost eighty years old. She still curls her hair, puts on makeup, and lays out a nice outfit to wear when going out. She's stunning, she's one of those women who always looks put together and well styled. Her name is Linda, it literally means *pretty* in

Spanish. But she doesn't feel that way. She doesn't see herself that way.

And so for as long as I can, and as often as I can, I will tell her how beautiful she is. She'll shake her head at me, or come up with some self-deprecating response about her hair falling flat or the laugh lines around her mouth, but I'll keep telling her anyway. Because she is my sunshine, and I never want to let her skies feel gray.

I'll love her enough for the both of us.

Maybe, one day, that hurt little girl living inside of her will heal enough to mend my grandma's wounds. I hope she does. I hope she steps out into the light, and my grandma can love herself the way she loves me. Because that love is extraordinary and worth sharing.

Until then, I'll love her enough for the both of us.

MONARCHS
Dedicated to my Grandma Rosie and Grandma Linda

My mama and my grandma

and the woman before-

she migrated north and fluttered some more.

With broke down wings and metal grill screams,

they beat and they bled to set me free.

Women drank the poison, toxins swimming in their veins,

all for me to end up soft, can't take no pain.

Took three generations to break their curse

just to die, but they laid their hope down first.

I try to carry their strength upon my back-

I'm flyin' south, flutters whisper all I lack.

Because of the women before, I will migrate-

I owe it all to them…they are my great.

Able to soar high, or at least I'll try-

leaning on their generation's borrowed traits.

NOT ALL HABITS ARE BAD

Over the years I've developed this habit of finding any excuse to run an errand. Oh, we're out of stamps? I'm on it. What's that, hunny? The water softener needs salt? Be back in twenty.

It's my mini escape disguised as a productive favor and I love it. I love choosing the radio station, cracking the window ever so slightly, and how magically seamless I can get in and out of my crossover without wrangling two adorable crocodiles out of their carseats. Probably the most habitual, I love calling my mom for our routine chat about nothing in particular.

Not all habits are bad.

Perhaps our calls would be less frequent if we still lived close to one another, but I have a feeling we'd still talk on the phone regularly. She was the hardest part of leaving coastal California...and if you've ever experienced the sun sinking into the majestic Pacific you understand the magnitude of that statement. Moving away from her feels like betrayal and loneliness and sometimes like a ghost limb. And when I became a mother a few years ago? Forget about it, that made the relocation all the more painful for both parties. These days our 1,900 mile distance is temporarily curtailed by the quick and casual catch up. If only for a few minutes it's like we're together in person, chatting over our morning coffee and toast.

What makes these phone calls even more special is the fact that she always picks up. Yes, I try to be mindful of the time difference, but she's a busy woman so in a way it feels like she's on call. For me. There's no one else in the world who's there for me like my mom, no matter how much I've grown. She's continued to be my beaming lighthouse, guiding me to a safe harbor when the seas become tumultuous. Because of this security I've been undeservedly awarded, I know how important it is to pay this forward. I surely hope that when my boys are older they know I'll always pick up the phone.

It's not lost on me that these almost daily interactions are a privilege. I have friends grieving the loss of their dear moms, and I ache for them and the bond that is now a memory. I know they dream about their mom's voice, and replay old voicemails just to hear her one more time.

There are women who grieve in a different sense, with mothers very much alive but maybe the relationship is strained or toxic. They'd give anything for the ten minutes of easy conversation I enjoy, and anything to have a mom like mine.

These brief chats about how Grandma is doing, or our plan for the next hair appointment, or whatever I'm currently irritated with (infinite possibilities) keep us connected with each other. The more mundane our conversation, the less it feels like I'm hundreds of miles away. I can't help but wonder if she realizes how special these phone calls are to me, and how much I cherish these snippets of home.

Come to think of it, perhaps my mini escapes aren't about leaving the house at all. Maybe this isn't about alone time (though yes, I do desperately need it). Maybe, just maybe, this habit of mine is about something much more significant.

So no, babe, I don't mind picking up your prescription. I don't mind at all.

LONG-DISTANCE GRANDPARENTS
Originally published on Her View from Home

You just finished another chaotic Facetime call. Chubby toddler fingers hung up several times, hoping to catch that elusive red button. He ran from his mom and your view was straight up that adorable nose for about half the conversation. His four year old brother alternated between refusing to talk and giving a doctoral lecture on carnivorous dinosaurs. You're a little frustrated. You're a little heartbroken. Frankly, you're a little dizzy from them running rogue with the phone through the house.
But you accept it. In fact, you cherish that crazy call because you are rocking a role you never imagined for yourself: you're a long distance grandparent.

It's not what you expected when you daydreamed of grandchildren, and it's certainly not the path you would have chosen, but that's life. The actuality that while you're physically here, your heart is beating a thousand miles away. You suspected trouble the moment your daughter brought that boy home, he had midwest charm and plans to return to the corn fields. She caught the kind of love that would follow him anywhere. And of course you were happy for her when they announced plans to marry and relocate, but the reality of that revelation brought you to your knees. Even years before those sweet little boys arrived, you wondered, "what about my future grandchildren?" You knew the weight of those words.

And now you're living within that reality. Sometimes it feels like you're confined to a screen and the occasional visit. You miss so many of the small, everyday joys that come with being a grandparent. And if we're being honest? It stinks. It stinks and sometimes (though you hate to admit it), you find yourself green with envy that the 'other grandparents' live so close. Wasn't it supposed to be the other way around? It doesn't feel fair. How will you establish a bond with your long distance grandchildren?

But it's there, I promise. It may not look the way you originally planned, but your bond is so evident it brings tears to my eyes. Mom and dad, even from afar you have brilliantly cultivated a relationship with my children that is cemented in love. I see it in the way you make the most of every call. I hear it in the way the boys cheer whenever there's a package waiting for them on our doorstep. I feel it in the way you hug them goodbye after a visit, their warm tears still dropping to my shoulders long after we've left. It's evident and it's real and it's a beautiful thing. To them you're not just their faraway relatives, you're grandma and grandpa.

Navigating this distance hasn't been easy for anyone. I can't count how many times I lamented living far away from home, remembering a painted rock from childhood. It said, "grow where you're planted." Oh how that rock taunts me! I didn't grow where I was planted- in fact I uprooted and took your dreams of living close to grandchildren away with my runaway branches. For that I am truly sorry. But I also firmly believe that love knows no distance. I think of the quote by Tom McNeal, "Distance means so little when someone means so much." My children may not live next door, but their love for you has strong roots. They have never felt less than your entire world, nor have they felt like they've missed out on anything because of the miles.

I always knew you'd both make exceptional grandparents, but to see it in action is awe-inspiring. Our circumstances may never change, but neither will my respect and appreciation for all you do for our family. For all you do for our boys. You are their Facetiming, frequent flier miles flying, constant group chat sharing, care package sending, memory making, forever loved and cherished, grandparents. And you are truly the best.

MADE FOR THIS

Mom, you were made for such a time as this. Always an incredible mother, there was never a doubt that your maternal light would shine even brighter the moment you became Grandma. Like Esther all those years ago, I believe you were knit by God for this purpose. To love and tend to your grandbabies.

And I've been blessed to be a witness of it.

I was able to witness your eyes water and fill as you heard that I was pregnant. It was like staring into years of hopeful prayers being answered.

I didn't even have to ask if you'd book a flight to be with me when the time came. I knew you'd be there.

And in that hospital room, you were by my side as my son came into this world. I was able to witness you behold him for the first time, to be one of the first people to hold him. As if you had been born for that moment.

When we brought the baby home, and I could barely walk or function, you leapt into action. I'll never forget the overnight oats you lovingly prepared. You made sure I ate them each morning those first few days. You made sure I had time to take a shower. You asked about my healing. You washed the pump parts while I struggled to figure out nursing. I was like a child again, and you took care of me while I took care of my own baby. You were made to nurture.

Like a true natural, you had sewn several blankets and towels for the baby. You had even brought pee-pee teepees. I hadn't even heard of them at the time! But that's what you were made for. To teach me about diaper changing and how to avoid flying streams of pee to the face.

I've been able to witness that little boy as he's grown up knowing the warmth and care of a grandmother's love. He's felt safe in your hugs, joy in your stories, and Jesus in your discipleship. And when his little brother was born, I know he felt extra special in your care while we were away in the hospital.

We didn't stop needing you when little brother came home, and I suspect we never will. Whether it's rocking a baby, giving advice, or just making sure my own basic needs are met, our family will always need your care. You were made to show up for us.

It just looks a little different now, witnessing you as a grandma as the boys grow. It's fewer snuggles and more wrestling on the living room floor. It means knowing that Leonardo is the blue turtle and Raphael is the one with the attitude. Being a grandma to little boys is learning about Pokemon and hearing about first crushes and more potty humor than anyone should ever have to endure. But don't worry, Mom, you were made for this, too.

GIVE ME FRIENDS WHO AREN'T KEEPING UP WITH THE JONESES
Originally published on Her View from Home

Following trends is nothing new. Long before Kitsch curls and Lululemon belt bags, there were perms and, well, the original Fanny packs. There's been a constant, circulating rotation of must buys for us to feel "cool" or relevant. And us women have been especially pressured to think we need these things to be accepted and part of the elusive 'village.'

Keeping up with the Jones' (or Kardashians for that matter) has just never been my thing. There's plenty of reasons why I'll never be called a trendy girl:

- I can't afford to be one
- I lack the stylish eye required
- I don't want to lose my originality

For those and other reasons, there have been a few circumstances where I couldn't quite find my place in those crowds. I couldn't keep up with the "it" looks or products. There'd be whispers about what other women were wearing, and they weren't complimentary.

Well I ain't buying it. Literally. And girl, you don't need any of those trends either to have my friendship.

Because even though style trends have been around for centuries, they seem to have escalated lately. We've become a cog in the consumerism wheel that makes us connect spending money to gaining acceptance. Not only do our clothes, hair, home, or car need to be presentable, now our cups too?! Okay, maybe the Stanley craze is what finally brought me over the edge about this! Must we have stylish *cups*?!

I mean, we used to drink water out of the garden hose, ladies. Remember? We don't need to get fancy with how we hydrate.

But I digress. This isn't about cups. Or eyelash extensions. Or the Kia Telluride that all of a sudden has become so popular you need to join a one year waitlist just to consider one. It's not about the stuff. It's about thinking you need the stuff to have a village.

That's not a village I want to join. I want the village that yells at my kids to check for cars before crossing the street. The one that includes back deck chats while the kids bounce on the trampoline. I want the village that tells me there's food in my teeth, and then tries to help me pick it out. The one that swaps clothes with me instead of buying new.

I'm lucky to say I've found that kind of village. It's a breath of fresh air, not to mention an ease on my wallet and peace of mind.

And if someone new comes along looking to join us, we'll care more about her heart and sense of humor than whatever the heck she's drinking out of.

To be sure, she could be clad in every designer trend possible, and we'd never judge her for it. So long as she's just as comfortable hanging in the front yard barefooted with her husband's sweat pants on. Because around here, we don't fuss.

And you shouldn't have to, either.

HOSTESS WITHOUT THE MOSTEST
Originally published on Her View from Home

I wasn't born a hostess. The idea of inviting people over to my home, whether planned in advance or on a whim, isn't a natural inclination of mine. In fact, knowing people are coming over usually fills me with a sense of dread and wet underarms. The predictable swarm of anxious questions would buzz into my ear while I frenzy cleaned:

Oh my gosh, what if the house has a weird smell I'm not aware of?

How the heck do you style a charcuterie board? Why did I think it'd be easy?

What if the house looks too messy? Or, alternately, what if the house looks too meticulous and people think I'm trying too hard to impress them? I don't want to come off as uptight…

You see what I mean? No one wants to be swapping brains with me right before company arrives, believe me. And let's be realistic, here. I know enough about being a human person that nobody is going to walk into my home and immediately start tracing a white-gloved finger over my baseboards or inspecting the organizational gravitas of my pantry. That's just not normal behavior. And I know that, rationally. But pre-hosting me is simply not a logical creature. I'm a mess.

Or I should say, I *used* to be a mess about hosting. And then I did something radical. And frankly, I tried something pretty dang risky. I started making a conscious effort to invite people over *more often*. I decided to train myself into feeling like a more natural hostess.

It was like I reverse psychology-ied myself. And the craziest part? It worked.

Hostessing is like any habit. It can be built and instilled with practice.

I didn't want to live in a world where I was afraid of inviting people over, and I certainly didn't want to wait until my home was 'perfect' enough to display. Because guess what? Our homes aren't precious masterpieces hanging in some snooty art gallery, they're tools to provide our family with safety and security. Homes aren't meant to be curated, they're meant to be shared.

So I stopped worrying about the look of my home and instead started to focus on its feel. I began to notice things that made me feel welcomed and cozy in the houses of others: plenty of throw blankets to share, a nice candle or diffuser, a host who was chill and just genuinely happy to see me. Those were the things I focused on, and they made all the difference.

Remember KISS- keep it simple, stupid? Yeah, that totally applies to hosting.

I'd invite the neighbors over with their kids, and order pizza. I encouraged our weekly Hike it Baby group to gather at my house for lunch after our walk. Inviting my kids' friends and their parents soon became no biggie after a few weeks of getting more used to the idea of simple hosting. Before long I was welcoming my husband's family over every Sunday for a standing dinner invitation. And when a few of us launched a women's group at church, I wasn't even surprised when typing my address as the first meeting location. It didn't need to be stressful anymore, because it had become a habit to open my home to others.

Because here's the thing, friend. It's not about the decorations of your home, or your charcuterie mastery (believe me, my charcuterie skills are *weak*). The people in your life who care about you just want to be invited into your life. And whether that means a bonfire in the backyard, or a festive themed night, or whatever your family would normally be doing anyways, it doesn't matter. All that matters is inviting people into your heart, by inviting them into your home.

Identity and Loss

CHASING MY FORMER SELF

ON MY MAT

OUT OF HIBERNATION

AMERICAN NINJA WARRIOR

SWEET, BUT BRIEF

BEFORE THE RAINBOW

CHASING MY FORMER SELF
Originally published on Her View from Home

Sometimes I yearn for her in the strangest of ways, teased but never fulfilled from a brief glimpse of her retreating shadow. I reach for her but again she escapes me. And I chase that feeling down, wanting nothing more than to return to what was but now is gone. I'm lunging after the woman I was before becoming a mother, but she doesn't exist anymore.

There are certain rituals of hers that are no longer mine to maintain. The spontaneity, the laziness, the selfishness...all ensnared in a whirring of freedom no longer attainable. The way a Saturday morning would slowly unfurl with a cup of coffee that stayed warm from first to last sip. Trips to run an errand were without a plan or packed bag. Clothes shopping was less about flattering and more about flaunting. Conversations were deep and distraction free, with rarely a mention of bodily fluids.

On especially nostalgic days, I try to replicate some of those rituals. The end result is sometimes satisfying, often drastically different from how its remembered, and always a cause for reflection. I begin to wonder if perhaps the ritual was always a shallow, fleeting joy rather than the elevated pedestal upon which it had been placed in my memory.

It's driving 45 minutes to another town so I can peruse the aisles of Trader Joe's without a grocery list, only there's a new love of mine strapped to my chest because he doesn't use bottles and we can't be apart for more than two hours. It's deliberately etching time in my day for yoga, but instead of going to a boutique studio I'm in my sweatpants following a yogi from the internet. It's asking my husband to run an errand with our toddler so I can tap into some much needed writing time, only to hear the cries of our baby minutes later, his monitor roaring over my thoughts.

Like reigniting a flame with an old love, my longing is accompanied with disappointment and fortunately a renewed appreciation for the present. I'm pulled back into the bigger picture and the new rituals of my life. It's the overwhelming pride of watching my child be authentically kind to someone who's hurting, without prompting. It's early mornings, in the quiet stillness of the nursery, nursing my baby while his free hand reaches gingerly for my face. It's finding community in ways I never knew existed, all unified by the shedding of our former selves.

Part of me will always miss who I used to be. But I know that, deep down, the best parts of her are still there, just beneath the surface. The rest of her, I'm ready to release. There's no use in anchoring to the weight of her dragging me down.

ON MY MAT

I consider myself a yogi. It's a loose title, very much unlike the sleek black pants that seem to feel tighter and tighter each year. But through various waves of commitment and zeal I have practiced yoga for about 14 years. It's been at times my exercise, therapy, rehabilitation...and at my worst, yoga has been my measuring.

In my early twenties I measured how I compared to the other participants in the room. Could I hold the pose longer than her? Why was she so much better than me? Who looks better in the mirror? Why am I sweating so much more than everyone else? Who does she think she is? Lululemon leggings, what is she, rich? Must be nice. Was anyone else able to hold crow as long? Where do I rank in this room of bending and stretching competitors?

The juxtaposition of the carefully crafted tranquil environment and my persistent inner turmoil sears memories of yoga in the early years. In the beginning, when life was without much responsibility or depth, my practice was in vain and vanity rather than the centering I so desperately needed. Yes, I was getting a good workout and stretch, but I was also constantly comparing myself to others. It was judgmental, ineffective, and the opposite of peace pursuing. I was hardest on myself, constantly critiquing every way I fell short. I think back on those hours in the studio and cringe.

And then I became a mom. Twice. It was after both the unmedicated, natural birth and planned c-section that yoga once again entered my life. I tiptoed back into exercise with trepidation. How could I exercise looking like this? When feeling so weak? I was embarrassed to be in a studio at first, so I started at home with youtube videos. It was almost a year after my second son was born that I walked back into a public yoga class.

The shift was immediate. I was a different person entirely from the woman who used to frequent this place. And it wasn't just motherhood that changed me, but rather a mix of maturity and confidence and inner peace slowly becoming restored through my walk with God. I was there to treat my mind and body, no matter where I 'ranked' among the fellow yogis.

The experience was ethereal. It was unreal how much more enjoyable the class was when I took my attention away from others, away from myself and just melted into the mat. Each stretch going deeper, each victory private, each stumble humorous. We were all there to better ourselves, and I was refusing to think any negative thoughts about myself or those around me. And when the instructor slowly invited us to final savasana, I let out an om that carried away years of comparing, shame, and judgement.

Is there an area of your life that reveals a broken or hurting side of you? I encourage you to reflect your intentions, and how your life can be improved with a shift in focus. Breathe in self love, breathe out doubt. Once more, breathe in strength, breathe out fragility. Namaste.

OUT OF HIBERNATION

There's been a reawakening of late, a gradual release from the hibernation of self that occurs during the postpartum stage of a 'baby year.'

It's subtle changes back to healthy eating and exercise, not because you feel like you SHOULD, but because you're no longer in survival mode and WANT to treat your body right.

It's making plans with friends you haven't seen in a while. The refreshing shift to a calendar that extends beyond baby visits and doctors appointments.

It's finally putting away the maternity clothes. I mean, the stretchy leggings are timeless but they're no longer a daily wardrobe staple.

It's reading for pleasure. Ah, the sweet serenity of reading just for fun. It's the first luxury to go when baby arrives and the ritual I cherish most when it returns.

It's genuinely, authentically, wholeheartedly enjoying your children and the time you have together. Not that you didn't during the newborn phase, but so much of that time is anchored to immediate necessities you may have lost the fun for a bit.

It's space for the question, "Who am I and who do I want to become?"

It's still putting the needs of others before your own, and it's still beating a servant's heart, but you're a little more YOU in the process.

I'd been reflecting on these subtle shifts the last few days when I found my favorite ring. It had been tucked away in the zipper compartment of my wallet from the morning of my C-section a few months ago. It seemed quite poetic to find it today. I'll wear it proudly.

AMERICAN NINJA WARRIOR

Have you ever watched something truly impressive and thought, 'Hmm, I bet I could do that'?

Oh, you haven't? Congratulations, you must be normal.

I, on the other hand, tend to fly on visions of grandeur. So when our family watched an episode of "American Ninja Warrior," naturally I convinced myself that being a ninja was a perfectly suited endeavor to take on.

I mean, how hard could it be, right? I am fairly athletic. Or, I used to be at least. And I love exercising and staying active. Everything felt aligned when I discovered that my small town in Eastern Iowa has a ninja warrior training facility that offers adult ninja classes.

I smiled at the description, "all ability levels welcomed." I could totally do this. And I totally *wanted* to do this; I began to imagine myself able to climb and fling and balance and soar in the sky with the greatest of ease. I could see it all unveiling before my very first class.

And then that very first class served a healthy dose of humility.

Be honest, you saw that coming, right? It's the story of my grace filled, failing forward life.

But that rough first class was exactly where the magic started to unfold. Because in that hour, as I wiped out on tumbling mats and couldn't quite climb the angled net and managed to get more chalk on my body than on my blistered hands, I let go of the expectation to be perfect. Or proficient, for that matter.

I laughed, picked myself up, and tried again. I chatted with the other brave souls, gaining camaraderie and a few tips on making it across the log roll (go sideways and FAST).

When I got home that night I told my family, "I could only do about 10% of that obstacle course, but it was fun!"

My boys were a little jealous they couldn't join (you must be six or older to use the facility), but they lit up when my stories of falling included a big grin on my face.

My husband congratulated me for trying. When asked if I was going to go back, my confirmation must've surprised him. Truth be told, I generally shy away from things I'm not automatically 'good' at. And I don't know if it's growing wiser with age, or motherhood, or just being ready to have some FUN, but for once I wanted to keep returning *because* I wasn't good at it. Yet. I'm very much not a ninja, yet.

And I may never become an American Ninja Warrior, but with each week comes new obstacles and new small victories (not to mention new blisters). I climbed the rope all the way to the top three times this week, something I wouldn't have even attempted before. I go into each class with a realistic goal. Sometimes it's to try something that scares me. Other times, I just want to get through a certain percentage of the course. I want to grow and open myself up to not being perfect, an expectation that always leads to disappointment.

Now when I watch "American Ninja Warrior," the level of admiration I have for those athletes is higher than the Bouldering Wall I faced a few classes ago. Not only do they have unparalleled brawn, balance, and bravery-they were once a beginner. They failed and flopped but they never gave up. And to me, that's the sign of a true ninja.

SWEET, BUT BRIEF

The night before the worst day of my life I had a dream. I dreamt my mom showed up out of nowhere, all the way from California, and handed me a box of tampons.

"But mom, I don't need these any more," I reminded her.
"Yes, yes you do," she had replied with a melancholic tone.

I woke to the sound of my alarm, signaling it was time to get ready for grad school. Only, I didn't make it to class that day. I instead woke up to spotting.

The spotting led to bleeding, and within an hour Ryan and I were sitting in silence in the emergency room. I went from only the day before proclaiming I'd only meet with female OB/GYNs to undressing behind a sheet in the company of a male doctor, nurse, and technician. My voice was shaky as I explained how far along I was, the events of the morning, how I wasn't experiencing any cramping so maybe that meant I was okay? Ryan was stoic, his body stiff with tension and concern. He respectfully looked away during the blood withdrawal, pelvic exam, and intravaginal ultrasound. With each test the results indicated the same conclusion, and with my feet still in the stirrups, the doctor gave us the probable news. The worst news.

There are so many odd things I remember about that morning, like frantically emailing my professor vague updates about being late and eventually absent from class, being embarrassed about bleeding on the hospital gown, praying to God His will be done, wondering whether to tell anyone about this when we hadn't even had time to share the good news yet. But what I'll always remember, and what also strongly stuck with Ryan, was when our nurse Brian put a gentle hand on my shoulder and with genuine sorrow gave us condolences for our loss. Because, as we experienced plenty throughout the recovery process, this kind of thing is fairly common and clinical; but what Brian gave us was not only comfort, it was what I'd come to crave- the recognition that our baby died. There was something so human and significant about this simple exchange, no empty promises or silver lining, no cold facts and numbers, just affirmation that our pain was warranted. I'll always be thankful for that.

Unlike many parents during a miscarriage, we were fortunate enough to get a possible reason: my blood type was incompatible with the baby's. Before that day, I had never considered that might be important, honestly I didn't even know what my blood type was. I was given an immune globulin injection to prevent this from happening next time. Next time? That day I couldn't fathom going through this pain again, but luckily Ryan followed up with questions about timelines and considerations. I was so short sightedly stunned I didn't realize that once I was ready to see the positives I'd also be ready to try again.

Deciding to tell close family and friends was uncomfortable but necessary. I've never been a private person, but even I had difficulty opening the conversation. The tone heavily depended on how I was feeling that day, truthfully, because in the weeks to follow my emotions and hormones were on a more turbulent coaster than normal. I went from weepy to straight-faced, from hopeful to worried. The one emotion I never felt, surprisingly to me, was bitter. I never struggled being around newborns or pregnant friends, because for a brief moment I understood what it meant to be a mother, and there's nothing I'd wish more than that feeling for the ones I love. In fact, what brought me to tears most often, was explaining the magnitude in which our lives changed for that short amount of time. But they weren't sad tears, they were tears of unconditional love. Because remembering the impact this baby had on us while in my womb was the concrete assurance that we'd give anything to sustain that kind of love and devotion.

I was not far along (about five weeks) when we lost our baby, and we only knew I was pregnant for four days before having to say goodbye. I realize more than ever how much worse it could have been, how attached thousands of parents become to their children before losing them. Chances are, we will one day have a perfectly healthy baby to love. But I wanted to share my experience, vulnerable as it may be, because for some reason miscarriage is not talked about. We all know women who have experienced them, and couples who struggle with having a child, yet it is taboo. Why? The best opportunities for healing (for me at least) was talking about it. I needed, and still need, to cry about it, to write about it, to pray about it, to share about it.

After four weeks, I know we will be okay. I'm learning to forgive and trust my body, to allow myself to be sad without relishing in despair. While on vacation I got a small wave tattoo, a reminder of what was lost and what is to come. To me, our baby was like a wave approaching the shore-vibrant and exciting, and gone just as quickly as it arrived. But like a wave, our journey is more than what I can see in front of the horizon:

Sweet, but brief-
A fleeting wave disappearing at my feet.

BEFORE THE RAINBOW

Four years ago I miscarried my first pregnancy. In that space of time there's been substantial healing. There's been a rainbow baby and his little brother. There's been reflection and processing and many, many conversations with friends who've suffered loss both before and after my own. Four years later and there isn't much raw pain like before. And yet, sometimes grief shows up.

Like when early summer arrives and the dates on the calendar gnaw at me like the gnats swarming with the humidity.

Like when I'm folding outgrown baby clothes to pass down, and I find the t-shirt I bought the day my blood test results confirmed the pregnancy. I shared our exciting news with my husband with that t-shirt.

Like when people joke about trying for a girl and I secretly wonder if I already lost her.

Grief can be blended with beautiful things, too.

Like when my boys are jumping on the couch and their squeals steal my breath. I feel so content, and I remember how four years ago I couldn't imagine this scene ever becoming true. Not for me, anyways.

One thing that's messed up about losing a first pregnancy is the nagging echo of wondering if you'll ever become a mother. What if that was my only chance? What's wrong with me? How can I ever be ready to try again?

Four years later, I can look at that broken girl and see a wonderful unveiling ahead for her family. But at the time? No, I couldn't find the rainbow while still standing in the storm.

If you're grieving a loss, there's no timeline for healing. And even when you think you've moved on, a memento or date on the calendar or picture will show up and disrupt you for a moment. But that's okay. Feel it, honor it, talk about it. And if you don't have a friend to talk to about it, seek someone out. There's many ways to become a mother, but you may need to seek shelter from the storm before finding that rainbow.

Praying Through it All

ABOUT THE AUTHOR

Photograph by Annalise Santillan

Brianna is an author living in Iowa with her husband and two sons. Between packing lunches and finding new nature trails, she is blessed to work in Christian ministry.